also by alberto ramos

eighteen

gay

lived written and illustrated by

alberto ramos

my rainbow people.

this
is for you.
i am in love with you.
i have always loved you.
this has always been about you.

contents

preface

gay
is a labor of love
in honor of the rainbow

letter to the rainbow people

my colorful. lives.
come sit here.
you are safe now.
take the weight off your shoulders.
rest your soul on these pages.
you are home now.
and my only request of you
is to use the beautiful word
that gives name to this book
to remember
for as long as the nights are cold
and the world against us
– we must keep on loving.

in deep love with you

Alberto Ramos

coming out

my heart flinches
every time i see a soul breaking
for showing itself how it is

— *coming out*

you tell me
you are nothing but a human disgrace
and hell has a spot well saved for your
unnatural gay ass

i hear
i wish i was
as brave as you are
to tell my world
to tell my parents
who i am
and
it did not matter
for me
to be nothing but a human disgrace
but a happy one
for them

— *compliment | cage*

it is not about understanding.
it's about
trying
to understand.

i am so tired
of coming out.
every morning
and
every night.
to come out
is all i ever do.
i change and
change and
change in the search
for myself and
i always end up
having to reintroduce myself
to the world
again.

(homage to becky albertalli's *love, simon*)

homosexuality.
is
an enduring
romantic
emotional
and/or
sexual
attraction.
towards those of
the same sex or gender.

— definitions

homophobia.
is
a degenerative disease
that
kills the human heart.
a form of fear
that disables
the individual who suffers it
from its natural ability to
sympathize
with forms of love.

— *definitions ii*

under the plain white walls.
where people of *faith*
teach us to be who we're not.
hit us to be who we're not.
humiliate us to be who we're not.
rape us to be who we're not.
kill us to be who we're not.
under.
the plain white walls we
die everyday. but can't help
to keep on breathing.

— *conversion therapy*

imagine being tortured until becoming what
you are not.
conversion therapy
is the practice of torturing a person
until they no longer recognize who they are.
through
chemical castration.
ice-pick lobotomies.
electric shocks (especially in genitals).
masturbatory reconditioning.
hard drugs.
and many other ways of torturing.
people are abused in an attempt to erase them
from their homosexual identities
in the search of their non-existent heterosexuality.
the real outcome is
chemically castrated individuals.
severely disabled individuals.
highly traumatized individuals.
suicidal individuals.
drugged individuals.
who are still gay.

— *conversion therapy is still legal and in practice in*
several countries over the 5 continents as of today

(an april saturday 2019)

the first time we loved.
so loud .
the moon could hear us.
we
woke up in blood
and a riot.

— stonewall inn. new york. june 28th 1969.

gay

when i think of the 50th anniversary of love.
of the rainbow.
on
a june dawn back in 1969.
i can't help but sharing the blood
of the millions who died for us to be. at peace.
of the millions who died for this book to be born.
and
i wake up in tears of love.

— *grateful | enraged*

your cruelty
is a poison
that
even if you spit it
(on me)
will always come back to your mouth.
will always
find its way back to
your mouth.

— origin

hidden.
in a clandestine pub.
and
in constant fear.
i will find love.

— *rainbow history*

beaten.
in a pool of my blood.
but
drowning in humiliation.
i will almost lose it.

— rainbow history ii

this is the dangerous thing about
being hated for just breathing.
you have nothing to lose.

— *win*

the very only thing
i ask for
if
i ever get killed in an attempt
of
being myself
is for the rainbow
to drink my blood
before
it becomes
colorless

— transfusion

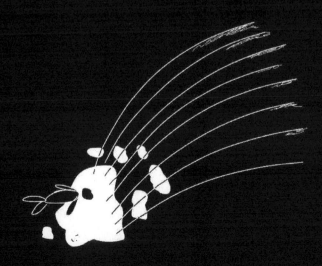

when you.
as a parent (teacher).
as an educator (teacher).
as a family member (teacher).
as a friend (teacher).
as a stranger (teacher).
teach a person
to disrespect.
instill the seed of hatred.
in the heart of their minds.
what do you exactly expect to happen.

— to raise on influence

if you have not respected. us. in certain ways. and
even have justified your lack of respect as a lack of
understanding. as if. you cannot respect something
you do not understand.

if you have not supported. us. in certain ways. when
it was most needed. because you refused to see what
was lying in the midst of your eyes. in front of your
very mind.

if you have not cared. about certain things. at certain
times. when it was due. as you had other priorities
that were more relevant.

that is totally okay. and it does not mean you did not
respect. support. or care at all. but you did not respect.
support. and/or care enough. or in the ways and places
it was needed.

— questions to your answers
in the form of answers to your questions

how are you going to teach me
to be brave when bravery
is so alien to your persona
how are you going to make me ambitious
if ambition is your all-time enemy
how are you going to teach me
how to respect if respect
is unfamiliar to you

how are you
going to preach me about love
when hatred is all you endure and
are moved by

— *example | incapacity*

do not become a war.
because
you want things to work.

— *remain*

if our mere existence
is a provocation for you
how can we live in peace

— the war for a decent life is the bloodiest of wars

day in day out
i get more lost
than found
in the words

— stereotype

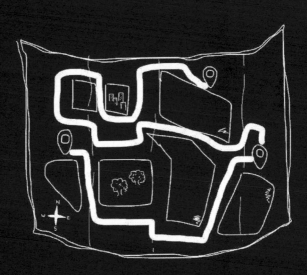

in what world
am i cruel
for exposing
cruelness
for stating
how cruel
you
have been
to me
to us

— *distortion*

if you want to
know what fear
has done to our
lives just look at
how many souls
are there still trying
to find love in violence
instead
of within them

— ultraviolence is a hidden heart

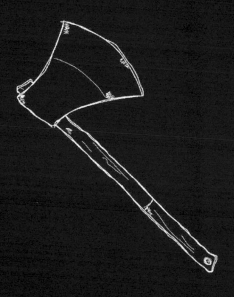

after turning not only schools
but whole educational systems
to your very preferences
after taking over the government
to impose your beliefs
after dominating the mainstream
the masses
from literature
to music industry
and media
to impose fear
making a business out of death
after bringing tens of thousands
of kids to their knees
not to pray
but for other evil things
they could not consent about
after threatening the lives of those
refusing to contribute to
your discriminatory ideology

you still have the nerve to claim
it is me the one who is indoctrinating
when i kiss my partner
in the midst of the street

— *religious dictatorship*

i'll
find love
in a riot.

love
will find me
in a riot.

these lives are never going to be left alone
at peace
until those
who have no idea what it is
to walk in these shoes
stop deciding
which shoes are better
for us
to walk on

— *the consequence to your incoherence is our death*

oppression
is a shadow
haunting me.
haunting us.

— poacher

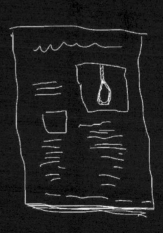

becoming the fighter or a number.

— *early decisions*

faith and/or religion.
are internal. and individual.
higher power to some translated as
god
energy
the universe
or other things of the kind
do not require churches nor masses.
that was humans adding that in.

therefore places of worship
that harm discriminate
or promote bigotry
are tainted.

— *the biggest delusion in the world*

never let their fear
of facing their truth
make you lose yours

— *find*

painful truths
are
also
truths.
are
the most
important
truths.

— salt

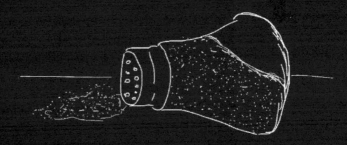

gay

do not give back to me
in private
what you took away from me
in public

— *hypocrisy*

i will not question your right
to have faith in something
that's none of my business
what i question is your intentions
of indoctrinating discriminatory beliefs
mask it as *education*
at the cost of millions of lives
and call it faith

— *cause it's a nonsensical lie and genocide*

homophobia and fear.
homophobia and hatred.
homophobia and stupidity.
homophobia and senseless.
homophobia and ignorance.
homophobia and emptiness.
homophobia and irrationality.
homophobia and latent homosexuality.
homophobia and homosexual tendencies.
homophobia and homoerotic sexual desire.

— synonym | mask

if i travel east. or south.
i feel the unsafest. all these weaponizing eyes trying
to devour me. all these laws ignorance hatred bigotry.
all their crosses. all upon me. out of nowhere. i can't
barely know where to find safe spots.

if it is north. i feel a bittersweet flavor which looks
innocent at times while at other times it begins to eat
me alive.

if however. i go west. i still can find all this
sophisticated hatred landing upon me. still see the
crosses trying to sink within me. it is this malicious
subtlety that scares me the most cause. i can't see it
coming. i can't see them coming.

these days. i don't even know where to go at all to
feel safe. to be. at peace. cause this hatred juice. made
some parts of me become a bit less human. a bit more
being. than the rest of us.

— *compass*

i want
to be rational and understanding.
but
i also want to be treated like a breathing thing.
a human heart.
because
when i am about to touch my rights
with my fingers
after all these years
looking for them
and
you slam them to the floor
spit on them. on me.
rational.
it is precisely what i can't be.

— patience isn't an endless resource

of course i am enraged
for thousands of years
the world has been drinking
all the blood out of the rainbow
and its thirst won't go away

to be so easily disguised
can be such a tragedy cause
one can't paint their skin tone
lighter or darker
to pretend to be what they're not
there's no other option but embracing it
be it full of love or self-contempt
neither can one as easily fool
about ethnicity race gender

but
it is
so incredibly
so terrifyingly
easy
for many rainbow offspring
to say you are
something you're not
and
to deny what you truly are
in
the process

— *rainbow's origin | pretending*

your raw homophobia (ignorance)
travels fast down my throat
but
it will be you
and not me
who will drown from it
eventually

the act of loving.

— *riot*

it has taken many lives.
so much pain.
and
so much love.
to birth this.
how
could it not touch you.

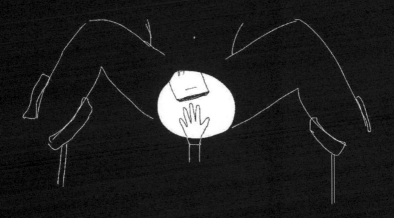

the very least
the rainbow people
deserve
if
they ever can't live their own lives
is to have the option to
read it
see it
feel it
elsewhere

— *representation*

i want to kindly ask my beautiful people.
from the rainbow.
to calm down
their
backstabbed hearts.
and
listen to these stories.

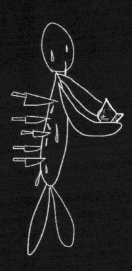

we need
more
rainbow literature.
rainbow movies.
rainbow series.
rainbow songs.
rainbow names.
rainbow people.
on the big cartels.
and
on the small homes.
on the schools.
on the camps.
on the parks.
on the streets.
on the brains.
this
urge of representation
is dying of thirst
and
all this lack of colors
are drinking us alive.

— *rain*

some cherish your light.
some hate to see your light.
some are afraid of your light.
some die of jealousy in your light.
some feel intimidated by your light.
some see their failures in your light.

— your light | because

kallman 1952.
heston and shields 1968.
pillard et al. 1981.
zuger 1978.
henry 1941.
bailey and pillard 1991.
kenyon 1968.
pillard and weinrich 1986.
kinsey et al. 1948.

are empirically relevant studies that argue through
a variety of methods (such as monozygotic twins
i.e. identical twins) why homosexuality is among
other things of a genetic predisposition. connecting it
so with darwin's essential work on evolutive biology
on the origin of species by means of natural selection
published in 1859. the biggest exponential of the
world-wide accepted theory of evolutionism.
and explaining through the survival of the fittest.
why homosexuality has preserved as an adaptive
behavior and not extinguished. because of the actual
advantages it provides to other individuals towards
reproduction and the preserve of the human species.

not only do the human species but a vast number
of others within the animal kingdom. practice
homosexual activities and behaviors since it
comes from their very natural instincts to do so.

there're also several records of homosexual behaviors.
in the form of literary works. mythographic materials.
art objects. among many others. from the ancient
greece to east asia and the native american. thousands
of years ago. free of judgment. before a crime against
nature. occurred. the biggest atrocity towards the
rainbow. ever committed.

church and religion. took over with the sickening.
terrifying. shameful. belief of homophobia. soon
instilling. with its enormous power. the disease
homophobia is. in the values of people. with the only
empirical evidence of a poorly translated book written
thousands of years ago. by who knows whom. hidden
in the safest place of earth. unavailable to the general
public. who so eagerly predict its distorted versions.

the only idea that two same-sex beings having an
emotional affective or sexual attraction is somewhat
wrong is simply hilarious in the eyes of science. the
ancient world. the animal kingdom. the theory of
evolutionism. and any being with a pinch of common
sense. but to church it goes against *nature*. and for
this matter i must admit i am utterly curious of which
nature they refer to. of which nature they belong to.

your
inability to realize
the pain you're causing
does not
exempt you
from accountability

i am
always dancing.
with you. for you.

— the lie

(homage to nayyirah waheed's *salt.*)

i am
always dancing.
with you. without you.

— *the truth*

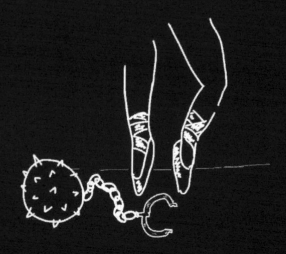

we choose to convert
our misery into
the next generation's delight
to project on them
not our suffering they should endure
but the empathy they shall become

this is how we teach to love

— *teaching is a compassionate act*

what is it to worry about.
if
the night will come
and
we'll be young again.

your mind
is the most attractive
thing at this place.

can you feel it breathing.

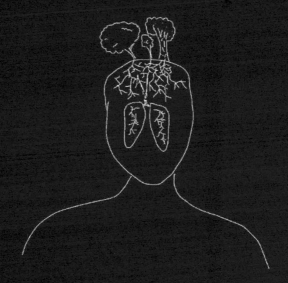

remember.
when you are water.
the boat lives on you.
for you.
because of you.
never the opposite.

— *host*

if you doing
what makes you happy
upsets your circle
all you must do
is find a new one

— changes

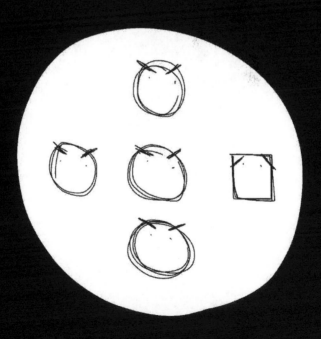

when i am told
hate the sin
and
love the sinner
i picture a bunch of white bouquets
a five-star buffet and
an orchestra of dancers
a celebration in the name of self-contempt
cause today is
the day
i marry my heartfelt pain

— *stockholm syndrome*

why
do you question my anger.
when it's solely fed off
your ignorance (fear).
as a gay man.
i have been oppressed
for as long as i can remember.
times of human lives worth less
than the pages of a book.
many lives of mine.
living. hidden.
how
would other reaction be more natural in me
than anger.

— *the law of action-reaction | the butterfly effect*

gay

this
poisoned love

— *hatred*

maybe.
you did not understand it
because
it
was not designed to be understood
by you.

— inclusion

the one history
that is often
the most forgotten is
the rainbow history

fighting and fighting and fighting
from coming in to coming out.
has consequences.

— *scar*

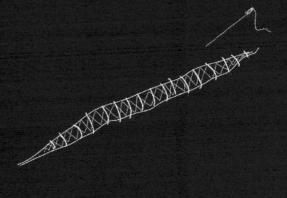

gay

i shall never have to choose between
being myself or living a decent life
being myself or not getting bullied
being myself or being successful
being myself or being respected
being myself or getting married
being myself or having a baby
being myself or getting a job

— *options*

to expose
the truth
in front
of their very eyes
won't be enough
for them to see it
if
they do not want to

— open

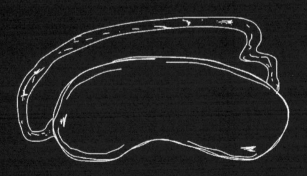

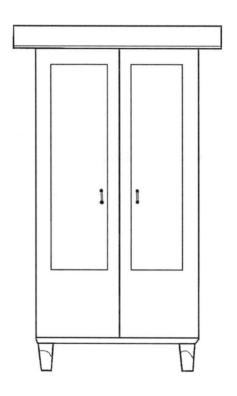

coming in

magic is
being raised to be invisible
but
becoming a storm of stars instead.

— coming in

a heart
a soul
and
a mind
must open themselves
first
for love to be

— *willing*

i am always
back
and forth
to the place where
irrationality
is the only rational thing

— traveling | homeland

it is guilt that drowns your veins.
nothing that i can fix.

— *medicine*

because we are tired of
listening. watching. living.
lives that are not ours.
stories
that are not ours.
told for us. made for us.
tired of having to translate it all
for it to falsely match what we are.

— belong

gay

after every line is crossed
all borders and boundaries
taken down and
you wonder
when was it
that you lost
where did you
leave yourself
when
they left

— *mourning oneself*

my people.
from the rainbow.
deserved this.

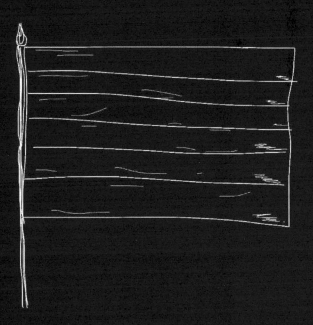

you should have known
every time you touch the rainbow
a person from there a color from it
the whole sky shatters and you
do not want to see mountains of
ignorance pushing their way to you
these waters roaring at the only memory
of all the times these colors were touched
with dirty intentions

you do not want to see this
do you

or maybe this
is exactly what you
came here to see

— *incitation*

i tend to find
myself
in the things i am
not

— heteronormativity

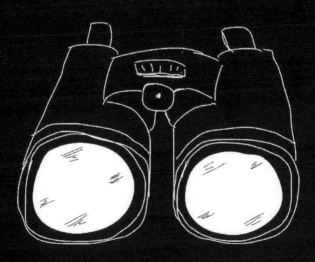

to keep a being alive
a dead breathing thing
does
not
mean
to take care of it

— *mental abuse*

the world spits in your face
who you are
everyday yet
you don't know

tell me dear
do you ever feel
locked inside yourself

it must be a beautiful winter thing.
to say *i like you.*
free. of fear.

— *the unknown privilege*

i am so close
and
so far
from home.
it is frightening.

— trans

now that you've ripped
my life in two
what am i going to do
with all your *sorrys*

alberto ramos

we
do not touch
out of fear

— contact | the straight friend dilemma

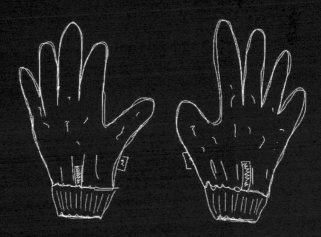

all along it felt as
if all i was surrounded by
were empty corps full of
mouths that spoke the more
the less they knew

alberto ramos

drunk
on love and fear
is how i
lose the last
sigh of love

to be told
at the place
that's supposed to
be a home to your heart.
by who is
supposed to
be the chest to your arms.
that
you should respect homophobia
because
it is just another way of thinking.

— *the definition of cruelty*

what if i
am sick after all
what if they're
all right and
i should but
not exist

— *delusion | forcing hatred juice into our throats*

even if you break me in half. time after time. this does
not. automatically. stop my love for you. it does not
drain it. even if i wish it did. some matters can't be
chosen as easily. i cannot adjust my feelings to my
own convenience. to what should or should not be.
unloving you. disconnecting you from my skin. is a
process. thus. you. hurting me. doesn't mean i do not
love you. although broken. disappointed. betrayed.
i love you. it's just a different type of love. not a pure
love. not a healthy love. not a proud love. but still
love. and although i am trying to learn how to unlove
you. how to get rid of whatever attaches me to you.
despite me not liking it. not liking you. i cannot deny.
at this moment. called present. i still love you.

— *sometimes emotions and people are complex*

how can we speak in
love when violence was
our mother tongue

we
do not always have to be
on our way
to become
the best version
of ourselves.
sometimes.
we need
to touch.
to explore.
our very worst parts.
for us to be sure what the
best version of us
really is.

will i ever find a home in
my own skin

— labor

i need time to close
time to heal
i have been a revolving door
a way for them to
come in and out
whenever it was
convenient

— *helping everyone can be a draining experience*

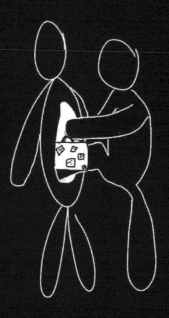

i am trying to unlearn what has been taught to me.
in the midst of this chaos. where no one is guilty for
anything but everyone has somebody to put the blame
on. i have been undoing. many lives within me. over
and over. what has been teared off this body since it
was ever created. this chaotic right to dignity i have
to presumably fight for.

i have been feeding my young heart. trying to process
the fact that. your soul is dying from starvation so
densely you can't help but vomiting all of your
prejudices. your viscera. so harshly upon me. i do not
want them to drown me. i do not want you. in my life.
i don't care how much of family relative friend or
anything you believe you are. i am learning. against
all odds. to be assertive. and if i cut you off in the
midst of it all cause not only you don't contribute to
my growth but you retain it. please. just take yourself.
entirely. anything left from you in these places.
and leave.

— *assertiveness*

if
i ever *expose* you.
it is not cause i care about
you.
doing this to me.
nor about what others
may think of you.
this is not about you.
this
is just me deserving to
live my truth.
out.
loud.
vividly.

when i am most ready
to listen to who i am
all
this senseless noise
won't let me hear a word

— *hateful noise | religious noise*

even
if you say sorry
even
if you mean it
i still need time
to heal a million
fires within me

— _forgiveness_

my skin breaks
but
it's your whole body that rains in blood.
cause we are family.

— empathy

if holding the thing you did
against the person you did it for
is your motif.
it is better you do not do the thing at all.

— *renting is not giving | dominance*

what is it with being
from the rainbow but
not talking about it
not showing what comes
most naturally from within you
what is it with hiding
your roots to be liked
or not to be disliked
to be safe or
not to be killed
what is it with hiding
the rainbow

— shame in the rainbow

gay

to be forced
to say who you are
when you're not ready to.
when you're not sure who.
when you do not want to.
cause so it will be easier.

for them.

— *an appeal to their noble motives. again.*
  at the cost of your mental health.

we have no words to find ourselves in.

— bath | ocean

gay

it has been a tough landing.
your presence in my lungs.
your heart in my chest.
your tears in my eyes.

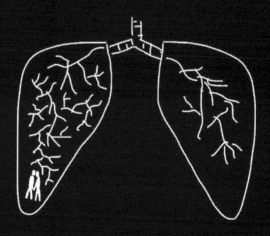

and there are nights in which i wish i was what i am
expected to. in which the fighting gets overwhelming.
there are nights. in which the pain fires a desire within
me. to rip off everything from me that makes me a
target. in which my heart is experiencing an anxiety
attack and all it needs is not having to fight
consistently for every breath.

sweet love. there are nights. when my lungs beg for
some air. and all i give them is resilience. oh my dear.
if only i told you about those nights. when my soul
leaves my body to begin playing around with my
blood. you'd be terrified. if i told you about the times
the soil eats itself under my feet and i can't help but
falling.

but when the morning comes. and i become a little
less human. a little more being. i like to see the sun
as my ally. a friend. as it lights up my face. i feel a
bit less lonely. a bit less hurt. under this shiny big
marvel. whose shine hides everything the night
holds. everything it implies. my love. some nights
are tough but. when the morning comes.
i feel stronger to keep pretending.

— *conversations with the moon*

sorry
can be
such a funny thing to say.
especially
if said
after destroying
every inch of life
in a corps.
after robbing
the last glimpse of decency
to a soul.
after breaking
the only piece of trust left.

— a word is not enough to repair this disaster

the world taught us best
blood is the red substance
running through our veins and arteries.
carrying oxygen and carbon dioxide.
that thing that waves in
and out
of our bodies when the hatred comes
and we show us as we are.
it taught us best
the red fluid can be seen in many
ways and forms.
and none of them means
unconditional love.

— unfamiliar fluids

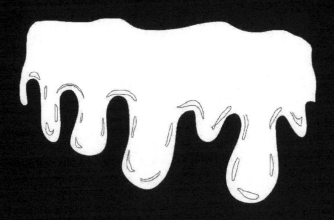

toxic masculinity is not:
- having a beer with the boys.
- playing sports.
- enjoying traditionally masculine things.
- having a beard.

toxic masculinity is:
- to be drown in and by your emotions for not expressing them.
- the idea that men cannot be single parents.
- assuming *real men* must always have a dominant role in a relationship.
- to be sexually aggressive.
- thinking that men cannot be victims of abuse and talking about it it's shameful.
- treating people (especially women or men with feminine traits) like sex objects.
- to be afraid to express yourself. emotionally.
- judging or abusing other men who don't display typically masculine behavior or traits.
- the idea that an attraction of any sort to themes strictly considered feminine mean the emasculation of a man.
- resorting to violence as an answer to everything.
- assuming any of the above is what a *real man* is or does.

sometimes fire flows
so naturally within me
i can't help but craving
a conversation about it
even when all i am
surrounded by are fake
lighters and wet matches

if everything i say you turn into an offence
tell me why
do you bother asking

— *or why should i bother answering*

i don't know
how to be me
in some places

— *allowed*.

gay

i wish someone
had taught me
as i grew up
that the rainbow
could also birth
stories
in book
film and
human form

— *upbringing*

i have drank
so much hatred juice
shot out of car windows
i think i am
becoming the ocean

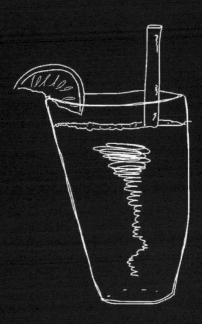

gay

i will teach my son
of love
when he wonders
how can i
be feminist and a man
how is it possible

milk and honey will drip
from my lips as i
explain to him
of course you can my love
the very first thing to
understand is
your emotions
are not
objective logic
unlike society taught you
and everything that disagrees with them
is not
a direct offense to your persona

— *the legacy of love*

(homage to rupi kaur's *milk and honey*)

the most null colorless and privileged
will try to hold your pen
to write your own story.
telling you about the issues
you have faced
and faced not.
about the things
you're entitled to suffer from
and the ones you're not.
about the pain.
of being you.

— homophobia for dummies

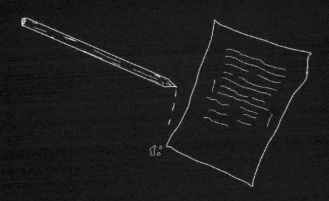

since birth
your child
is helplessly starving for
education.

feed them.

— *nutrition*

if it is not rainbow blood
that runs through your veins
who are you to speak
in the name of rainbow's tears

— be

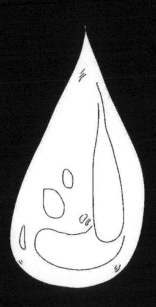

to undo the curse
of expecting the very worst
from everybody
because that is exactly what
they've always given to you

— *sequel*

some nights
the world sips
all the water from my mouth
and i can't help
but becoming the sea

— *osmosis*

gay

your thirst for public acclamation
shouldn't play a role
in our everyday fights
we're happy
that your vacation
to the less privileged land
was a satisfactory one
but it is not
your
land
and this is not
your fight to represent

— fake | taking advantage of the rainbow

i want
rainbow actors playing rainbow characters.
rainbow stories told by rainbow storytellers.
rainbow issues treated by rainbow speakers.
rainbow love represented by rainbow lovers.

— real | context

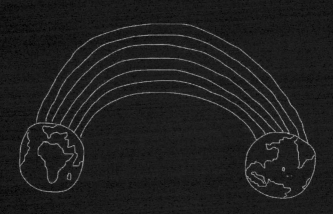

before you play the role of being offended by nothing
i hope you remember
when she tried to get away from him
and he forced a kiss into her lips.
when she tried to leave
and he held her wrists.
when she tried to reject him
and he attacked her.
or
when he tried to ignore her
and she smacked his butt.
when he rejected her
yet she caressed his chest.
when he blocked her
but she kept insisting.

cause outside of the rainbow
boundaries are ignored all along.
empty bodies abruptly. violently.
forcing their way to you.
but here at the rainbow
we. are being judged. threatened. insulted.
for smiling and staring. *too* long.

— *double standards*

alberto ramos

i had almost
forgotten.
thank you.
for reminding me
who
you are.

— *betray*

tell me love
did you find them in my shadow
did those beautiful faces
ever fill the empty holes that
were left all over you
after my leave
did they ever touched your mind
speak to your mind
hold your mind
the way i did

— *the things only i could do (to you)*

i have always been
a minefield.
of butterflies.

perhaps you think it is
the longing for empty sex
but in reality it is simply
an eternal quest for warmth

— *shortage*

still don't know if
i remember you when i feel hurt
or feel hurt when i remember you

gay

i want a friend whose chest i can lie on when mine
can no longer hold the anxiety. the pressure beating.
having arms to fall in when life falls apart and so do i.
a being to hold to trust and to feel asleep with out of
comfort. peace. someone not frightened to caress and
kiss me when i need the warmth. simply. a place in
human form. to call home. to feel safe. is it too much
that i'm asking for. to have a second breath. without
fear of love.

— *i want friends not scared of my sexuality*

my honesty
is
wild salt
in your eyes
sharp rings
in your eardrums

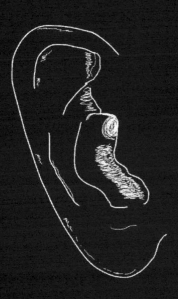

gay

it's been
eighteen years
drunk of homophobia juice

i am sorry
if i still vomit some of it
on you
every once in a while

— *detox*

and again. you wake up in tears of love. of joy. of
fear. of anger. of frustration. deciding it's you that's
the problem. thinking of every unchangeable part of
you that you wish could just be ripped out of your
soul. you want to look like the ones they like. even
when neither your legs nor your body hold what they
hold. but what does that matter. when at this point
you're not interested in anything that's not
straightforward unfair. unreachable. to you.

or in the best days. you feel renewed and positive.
and you even ask yourself if their curiosity of you
could be the best that could happen. even if it's by
mistake. cause you'd happily be theirs. just to be
anything. remotely related to love and be loved. in
a world. designed to make that feeling so specially.
specifically. hidden from you.

> — *rainbows in small towns of little options*
> *(falling for a straight person)*

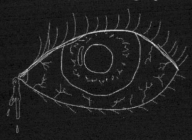

all the women and
men living within me
are exhausted and terrified

it is tiring
the very idea that
us evoking any contact
is somehow a reason for them
to question their sexuality

and it is frightening
to be fully misunderstood
and labeled as evil when
all we want is light

how naive it was of you.
to think
i turned off.
when i was only saving
my light.
to become the moon.

— *immortal*

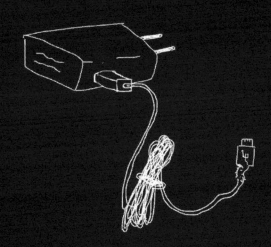

what does it mean.
if i can hold my heart high
despite dripping blood
from a hundred knifes.
stabbing my soul.
but
the only touch.
of one knife.
the mere smell.
of blood.
makes you faint.
do i deserve less comprehension.
for being used to the suffering.
do i deserve less love.

— *fair*

i think
one of the
best and
worst parts
of being gay is
that it can
be hidden

not everybody can lie and
deny who they are so easily
when it is convenient

not everybody can remember
to love who they are when it
can be so easily forgotten. hidden.

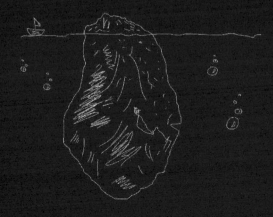

gay

what to do
when everything i am
is a controversy

— *embrace yourself tighter*

tell me
my old love
did you learn to love her
as they said you would
did she ever taste half as good
half as genuine
as i did
look at me in the eye
and tell me
you can't help but thinking of me
when the two of you
make an attempt of love

my sweet love. there hasn't been a single day out of
my life when i haven't thought of you. of us. even if
it's in another bed. in other arms. no one has ever
replaced the warmth of your chest. no one ever made
me feel the air. this life. so densely. as you did. no
other lips. no other body. have fuel my inner fires so
lively. as you did. oh baby. but look what the world
has done to us.

sometimes i wonder what would have been of us.
had we chosen freedom over fear. sometimes. i think
of what would they say. what would my wife think.
how would my children react. if they knew the only
time i felt alive was when you whispered all the future
we had together in my ears. softly. i wonder if it was
really worth it. to risk our lives at the expense of
living them. or living dead inside in exchange of
staying alive. my love. is it too late to tell you
that i regret my choices. that i am sorry.

to tell you i despise the fact these have been my
selfish worries. that panic has been my only friend
ever since our lips touched. i am sorry it has taken
too long for me to assimilate my feelings for you.
to understand it is a blessing to feel love despite what
they say. i am sorry i cannot undo what i have done.
i cannot rebuild what i have destroyed.

and now all i have left are the things we shared. and
the million lives we lived in a couple of moments.
that are now fighting so desperately to come out of
my chest. calling out so loudly. so vividly.
in the quest of you.

right now. and forever. all i have left in this world of
us. is this letter. written with the grief of my blood.
may it find its way to your hands through the sea
of tears i have left behind me all these past years.
alongside our photographs. and our memories. my
darling. for they are the only place where we could
ever be safe together.

— letter to the love of my life

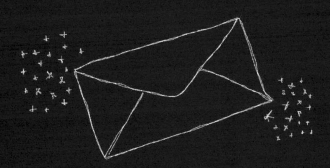

gay

i want a soul
that expands.
and contracts.
that grows each and
every time.
that jumps
in excitement.
i want a body that feels.

— *when the pain comes*

she
still lives
if you can hear her

— hope

sometimes
i wish i could just
sleep on his soul
not feeling
like sex is the only
beautiful thing
that
could happen
when
i lay next to his breath

— *romantic*

my
love.
you were a before and
after.
and
everything that comes
after you
will belong to a parallel life.
people moments pain
will all belong to
a life i wish was not occurring.
i wish
was not my life.

— *what fear has done to our lives (to our loves)*

(homage to andré aciman's *call me by your name*)

if
you do a thing for another.
something for something.
and
use the thing you did
as a weapon
in the face of whom you did it for.
if
exchange is the only way
you know of love.
you
do not know
what love is.

— *power*

even if it's
just for tonight.
even if we
don't ever let the world know.
even if you
are all the world i
want to know.

— *us*

it is not the same
telling you what
i think. (you are)
than
telling you what
i think. (you can handle)

— *hardcore truths*

i want
i need
to host your body in mine

— tenant

when
you lay
next to me
under me
in me
for me
inside of me
this
is who you are
the rest
is incidental

— reveal

i have never felt
so lost.
so found.
as i do
when
the night comes
and
you speak softly.

— *intimacy*

i have always belonged to you
just as
you have always belonged to me
it was just
the time
the fear
the hatred
that drew us so apart
we ended up
belonging to others

— *reality*

your mind
is your best friend
and worst enemy
it is responsible
for holding you back
and pushing you forward

— *proactive*

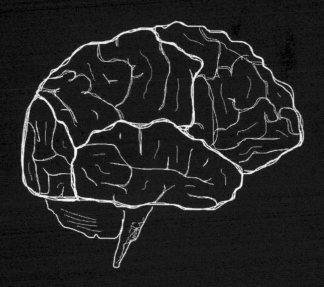

last night.
in my wildest waters.
i dreamt of you.

— *drown*

don't ever stop being
a storm of stars
just to comfort the
jealousy of a match

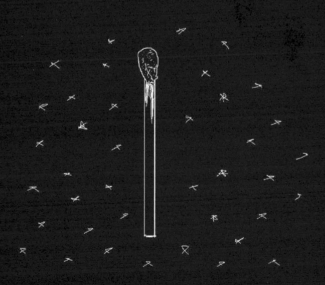

gay

i am rooting.
drawing.
pouring.
my way
back
to you.

i can't help but blooming
upon hearing your breath

— heal

gay

this
electricity
within me

with your fingers.
under the sky.
feel me.

— *constellations*

come.
inside.
take off your life.
rest your soul.
put your hands.
on my moon.

— *home*

you can always talk to me.
i am your mirror.
your light and shadow.
a hand to your hand.
warmth for your chest.
your homeland.

— community

please. talk about yourself. i'll listen to every detail.
the only sound of your voice got me sat down with
my elbows held on the table. these butterflies on your
chest. listening to every and one of your interests. of
your goals. what upsets you. what moves you. what
drives you crazy. i want you to feel like these ears are
a safe place for your comfort. a home to your heart. to
make you feel so genuinely loved and admired. as you
are. your stories. your spirit. your life. are of major
importance—if you mind me saying so. you're the
brightest ray of light that the sun ever birthed. and
this sincere appreciation. is not empty flattering.
but a reminder of the beauty living within you.
in case you ever forget.

— you

if you want to.
tonight.
we
could break into stars.

— catharsis

gay

i want you
to touch me
in this place
between always and never

— *spacetime*

the moment i grew up
didn't come from the day i was born
but from the day i allowed myself
to understand others
and their view-points
instead of evaluating them

— a happier place

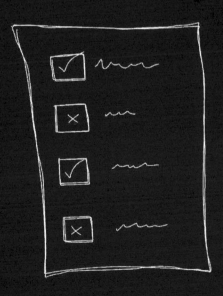

gay

the things you think and feel
you have only felt yourself—
believe me
i have survived them already
through blood sweat and tears
these
are our everyday battles

— *together*

alberto ramos

at
night.
in the middle of
my oceans.
dive into me.

— swimming in space

that one thing
i am
among a million others
is a gay man

speaking of
that one thing
i am
among a million others
does not mean this
is the only thing i am

— *fragment*

mirrors come to my rescue
i break myself as they shout
together or apart
better or worse
here or away

it has always been you

gay

my baby.
do not bother explaining.
they would never understand.

alberto ramos

project on them the light
you want them
to become

— teacher

there is an infinite line
of
lives.
sexes.
genders.
between
being.
feeling.
living.
as
girl or boy.

— *identity | non-binary*

a boy
is not necessarily a boy.
because
of being born boy.

a girl
is not necessarily a girl.
because
of being born girl.

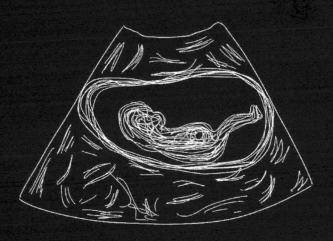

when
my behavior as a boy/girl does not
match how regular boys/girls should behave
according to society.

— this is gender disconformity

what
i perceive myself as.
whether it is a masculine. girl.
or a feminine. boy.
anything i identify myself with.
my very right to perceive my own gender
subjectively.

— this is gender identity

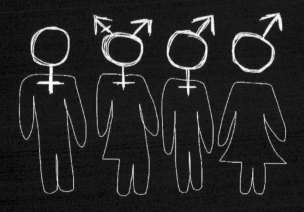

when
i am helplessly at war
with my gender identity and birth gender.

— *this is gender dysphoria*

when
i was simply and plainly
born to love. to feel attracted to people.
in a lasting way. whether it be
affective. romantic. sexual. or psychologically.

— this is sexual orientation

had you spent
reading.
all this time.
you spent
hating.
today
you'd be something extraordinary.

— *priority*

alberto ramos

gender
and
sex.

— *distinction*

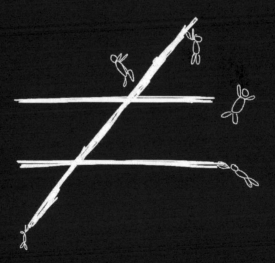

do not ever
get stuck in their vision.
do you hear this.
this
is not
who
you
are.
meant to be.
never
listen to their fear.
in the middle
of their very waters.
break yourself free.

— *blind*

alberto ramos

to feed your soul.

— poetry | purpose

dear world.

i've had enough.
these past weeks. months. years. this past life. have
been too challenging on my young feet. i don't even
know how when nor whether to say goodbye.

the ones closer to me have hurt me the most. which is
funny because they'll most likely think otherwise for
the rest of their delusional lives even despite of this
letter. how curious it is. how selfish. how a person
can see you everyday falling apart in front of their
very eyes. and not suspect they may be capable of
providing something else rather than judgement
and pressure.

i have been trying to figure things out. to have a place
to call heart and perhaps a soul to call home. i have hit
all rock bottoms i ever thought i'd possibly could. and
it all now led me to think. if life was automatized. if
only it was fair. you and i would be far apart from
each other. free of pain. it was the smallest things
that sank me the most when they were multiplied
by a thousand.

i couldn't possibly know if another life awaits for me
after my departure in this one. a life where i would be
treated equally. a realization after a long nightmare
that would give me the chance to start anew. to live
as decently. as everybody else did.

if only i got this chance. to be who i wanted. to
love who i wanted. free of punishment. humiliation.
sorrow. what i do know is i've had enough already.
and my soul cannot wait for the healing anymore
while everybody is ripping it to pieces day by day.

i no longer want to live. my lungs have inhaled so
much hatred even if i wanted to. my respiratory
system denies to keep breathing. i doubt what is
about to occur could be any worse than what is
already helplessly happening. and although scared.
i am also thrilled. for i might today for the first time
in my life. find myself. in peace.

— letter of goodbye to a life of disgrace

my baby.
pure
intense
beautiful
offspring of the rainbow.

even though. life has been so hard on your feet. for
these past weeks. months. years. even though they've
hurt you. they're hurting you. and they'll most likely
hurt you. this is not the whole story. do you hear me.
this is a scene. a very tough one. probably the most
painful you'll ever live. in the tale of your life.

this. is the story you'll grow out of. one for the books.
the story you'll remember with a nostalgic fever and
a little punch in the chest. the one that will make you
mature and see the big things as a still small being.
the pain will harden your soul so that you become
stronger and invincible. but loving and generous too.

this is the teaching life gives you. the teaching you
give yourself. because in spite of this cruelty you're
being forced to swallow. someday. when digested.
when you're at a better place. away from here.
far from the shadow. you will realize this. was not
permanent. not life. but temporary. circumstantial.

do not ever forget the most important relationship
of your life. do not ever forget yourself. i know.
especially when young. your spirit is so wild and
vivid that when things go wrong it feels the world is
trembling. but it truly is just a phase. a stage made
from a combination of negative factors. negative
surroundings. negative spaces. negative time. for you
right now. which will be a mere memory sooner than
you think when you're out there chasing and living
your biggest dreams. full. of live. breathing loudly.

no matter how hard they try. do not ever let anybody
make you feel like you don't deserve a life full of love
and respect. your light is still here. it is them who did
not learn how to see it without blinding themselves
and therefore attempting to turn it off. and making
your essence disappear. won't ever be the answer.
so please know. every part of me. believes in
every part of you. i love you. keep going.

— letter of hope to an up-coming life of joy

gay

i am so frankly thankful
that i did
that i've dared
to do it
it
has changed my life

— loving myself

and
what about the art of
saying *no*.
no. i do *not* like you.
no. i do *not* want to do that.
no. i do *not* want to date you.
no. i do *not* want you to touch me.

— politeness | a proper education

forgive. you.
when you fill the most lonely. and desperate.
parts of yourself. with the wrong energy.
at the wrong spaces.
in the worst ways.

i know you had to.
that
this was better than remaining empty.

forgive. you.
for leaving behind the wrong energy
spaces and ways.
when you are at a better place.
because
it no longer serves you either to grow.
or not to sink.

gay

i am.
despite of you.
not because of.

— *nuance*

i have grown between short circuits.
and
now i am a storm of stars.

— epilepsy

to be honest
is not
to be cruel.
and
to be cruel
is not
to be honest.

these flowers that come out of my mouth
as i speak.
this is my mother tongue.

my truth is
my greatest gift.
my most powerful weapon.
it is
the most valuable treasure i carry.
within.

— *freedom*

alberto ramos

in pure souls it waves
its way out for free
but it costs millions
for those living in fear

— *the truth and its taxes*

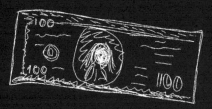

this is not a journey of being solely defined
by your sexuality
instead
this is a journey of bravery
of learning to love
what you were forced to grow ashamed of
of being proud to live as you fully
of finding comfort in your skin
as you are
becoming aware of every piece of your being
making it yours
personal
representative
to embrace a beautiful part of what makes you
you

— *more*

always
be kind to your art.
listen to its tears.
heal its soul.
put it out.
break it.
free.

— protect yourself | criticism

i am accountable.
for
putting the breath of my soul
in my art.
but if somebody chooses
to misunderstand the light.
to think low of the light.
to distort the light.
that is not my problem.

— *responsible*

i am
never
lonely.
if i am
in company
of myself.

— crowd

today i want to take a moment to appreciate all of the things i have. in life. to appreciate this time. this air. this reckless breeze running through my veins. i want to pause. to breathe. and to apologize. to myself. for comparing myself. for comparing my path. to others. especially for comparing me with those who were given opportunities and means i had to create myself.

i want to apologize to myself for preaching so intensely what i sometimes find myself unable to endure. for not allowing me to take my own time to heal. for giving it to others instead. i want to apologize. first and foremost. for treating every morning as an earned fact and not a gift. as if i couldn't lose it all today and not wake up tomorrow. alive. i am sorry for not being how thankful i should be for all the things i have. all the things i am.

and even though i'm afraid i might take life for granted again. i hope i find the courage. the time. and above all the willingness within me. to start all over again. free. of guilt.

— here is to a life full of light and free of guilt

i am complete.
i have always been
complete.
and
if there's one single thing
i am sure i will always be
is complete.

—*full*

i am coming home.
from
and
back
to myself.

— *journey*

about the author

alberto ramos is the young author and illustrator of
two collections of poetry. his first work *eighteen* was
written and published in 2018 during his high school
years in sweden, expressing his torture as a gay teen
at a highly conservative and orthodox place. although
alberto's first work refers mainly to his experiences
in stockholm, where he studies, ramos is originally
from málaga, spain. *gay* is the second volume to *the
eighteen series,* a series that explores the dark and
bright parts of alberto's experiences with bullying
abuse loss depression trauma homophobia and self-
love as an eighteen-year-old. during his martyrdom,
ramos attracted the attention of several european mass
media platforms with his artistic projects and his way
of dealing with the abuse he was enduring. ever since,
alberto has lectured and performed his work *eighteen*
to audiences across many cities around the world.

important information

whenever you feel the weight on your back is too much to handle. life's too rough. it isn't worth to be alive. your breath becomes so heavy you begin to think of putting an end to your life. as soon as any of those thoughts (no matter the intensity) come to your beautiful mind and you have no way to vent nor see a solution. please call.

argentina: **02234930430**   australia: **131114**

austria: **017133374**   belgium: **106**

botswana: **3911270**   brazil: **212339191**

canada: **5147234000**   croatia: **014833888**

denmark: **70201201**   egypt: **7621602**

estonia: **3726558088**   finland: **010 195 202**

france: **0145394000**   germany: **08001810771**

holland: **09000767**   hong kong: **2382 0000**

hungary: **116123**   india: **8888817666**

ireland: **8457909090**   italy: **800860022**

japan: **352869090**   mexico: **5255102550**

new zealand: **800543354**   norway: **81533300**

philippines: **28969191**   poland: **5270000**

portugal: **21 854 07 40**   russia: **0078202577577**

spain: **914590050**   south africa: **0514445691**

sweden: **317112400**   switzerland: **143**

united kingdom: **8457909090**

united states: **18002738255**

if you are homosexual. bisexual. lesbian. trans. queer.
pansexual. asexual. and more. you can text and call
here.

(+1) 1-866-488-7386

i love everything you are.

the eighteen series

eighteen is alberto's first book, and serves as the
opening of *the eighteen series*. it is a collection of
poetry and prose that quickly became a #1 bestseller.
gay is ramos' second work and second volume of
the eighteen series. alberto's labor has eluded great
praise and interest in huge media platforms and
public figures and his story as well as his debut
work *eighteen* have been largely discussed in political
contexts, being his work used in a variety of european
universities to raise awareness on the important issues
it deals with.

the visual journey

alberto uses social media to represent visually
the pages of *the eighteen series*.
to watch it be, follow it here:

instagram & twitter: @albeertoramos

Made in United States
Orlando, FL
28 March 2022

16245638R00120